Aesop's Fables 2

Aesop's Fables 2

Aesop | Arthur Rackham

THE CLASSIC

contents

1. The Wolf and the Kid

There was once a little Kid whose growing horns made him think he was a grown-up Billy Goat and able to take care of himself. So one evening when the flock started home from the pasture and his mother called, the Kid paid no heed and kept right on nibbling the tender grass. A little later when he lifted his head, the flock was gone.

He was all alone. The sun was sinking. Long shadows came creeping over the ground. A chilly little wind came creeping with them making scary noises in the grass. The Kid shivered as he thought of the terrible Wolf. Then he started wildly over the field, bleating for his mother. But not halfway, near a clump of trees, there was the

Wolf! The Kid knew there was little hope for him.

"Please, Mr. Wolf," he said trembling, "I know you are going to eat me. But first please pipe me a tune, for I want to dance and be merry as long as I can."

The Wolf liked the idea of a little music before eating, so he struck up a merry tune and the Kid leaped and frisked gaily.

Meanwhile, the flock was moving slowly homeward. In the still evening air the Wolf's piping carried far. The Shepherd Dogs pricked up their ears. They recognized the song the Wolf sings before a feast, and in a moment they were racing back to the pasture. The Wolf's song ended suddenly, and as he ran, with the Dogs at his heels, he called himself a fool for turning piper to please a Kid, when he should have stuck to his butcher's trade.

Do not let anything turn you from your purpose.

2. The Fox and the Grasshopper

A Grasshopper sat chirping in the branches of a tree. A Fox heard her, and, thinking what a dainty morsel she would make, he tried to get her down by a trick.

Standing below in full view of her, he praised her song in the most flattering terms, and begged her to descend, saying he would like to make the acquaintance of the owner of so beautiful a voice. But she was not to be taken in, and replied, "You are very much mistaken, my dear sir, if you imagine I am going to come down: I keep well out of the way of you and your kind ever since the day when I saw numbers of grasshoppers' wings strewn about the entrance to a fox's earth."

The wise learn from the misfortune of the others.

3. The Foxes and the River

A number of Foxes assembled on the bank of a river and wanted to drink; but the current was so strong and the water looked so deep and dangerous that they didn't dare to do so, but stood near the edge encouraging one another not to be afraid. At last one of them, to shame the rest, and show how brave he was, said, "I am not a bit frightened! See, I'll step right into the water!"

He had no sooner done so than the current swept him off his feet. When the others saw him being carried down-stream they cried, "Don't go and leave us! Come back and show us where we too can drink with safety." But he replied, "I'm afraid I can't yet: I want to go to the seaside, and this current will take me there nicely. When I come back I'll show you with pleasure."

Those who bluff always call for the dangers.

4. The Cock and the Fox

A Fox was caught in a trap one fine morning, because he had got too near the Farmer's hen house. No doubt he was hungry, but that was not an excuse for stealing.

A Cock, rising early, discovered what had happened. He knew the Fox could not get at him, so he went a little closer to get a good look at his enemy.

The Fox saw a slender chance of escape.

"Dear friend," he said, "I was just on my way to visit a sick relative, when I stumbled into this string and got all tangled up. But please do not tell anybody about it. I dislike causing sorrow to anybody, and I am sure I can soon gnaw this string to pieces."

But the Cock was not to be so easily

fooled. He soon roused the whole hen yard, and when the Farmer came running out, that was the end of Mr. Fox.

The wicked deserve no aid.

5. The Stag and the Lion

A Stag was chased by the hounds, and took refuge in a cave, where he hoped to be safe from his pursuers. Unfortunately the cave contained a Lion, to whom he fell an easy prey. "Unhappy that I am," he cried, "I am saved from the power of the dogs only to fall into the clutches of a Lion."

Out of the frying pan into the fire.

6. The Lion, the Wolf, and the Fox

A Lion, infirm with age, lay sick in his den, and all the beasts of the forest came to inquire after his health with the exception of the Fox.

The Wolf thought this was a good opportunity for paying off old scores against the Fox, so he called the attention of the Lion to his absence, and said, "You see, sire, that we have all come to see how you are except the Fox, who hasn't come near you, and doesn't care whether you are well or ill."

Just then the Fox came in and heard the last words of the Wolf. The Lion roared at him in deep displeasure, but he begged to be allowed to explain his absence, and said, "Not one of them cares for you so much as I, sire, for all the time I have been going round to the doctors and trying to find a cure for your illness."

"And may I ask if you have found one?" said the Lion.

"I have, sire," said the Fox, "and it is this: you must flay a Wolf and wrap yourself in his skin while it is still warm."

The Lion accordingly turned to the Wolf and struck him dead with one blow of his paw, in order to try the Fox's prescription; but the Fox laughed and said to himself, "That's what comes of stirring up ill-will."

The first liar doesn't stand a chance.

7. The Crow and the Pitcher

In a spell of dry weather, when the Birds could find very little to drink, a thirsty Crow found a pitcher with a little water in it. But the pitcher was high and had a narrow neck, and no matter how he tried, the Crow could not reach the water. The poor thing felt as if he must die of thirst.

Then an idea came to him. Picking up some small pebbles, he dropped them into the pitcher one by one. With each pebble the water rose a little higher until at last it was near enough so he could drink.

In a pinch a good use of our wits may help us out.

8. The Crow and the Raven

A Crow became very jealous of a Raven, because the latter was regarded by men as a bird of omen which foretold the future, and was accordingly held in great respect by them. She was very anxious to get the same sort of reputation herself; and, one day, seeing some travellers approaching, she flew on to a branch of a tree at the roadside and cawed as loud as she could. The travellers were in some dismay at the sound, for they feared it might be a bad omen; till one of them, spying the Crow, said to his companions, "It's all right, my friends, we can go on without fear, for it's only a crow and that means nothing."

Those who pretend to be something they are not only make themselves ridiculous.

9. The Parrot and the Cat

A Man once bought a Parrot and gave it the run of his house. It revelled in its liberty, and presently flew up on to the mantelpiece and screamed away to its heart's content.

The noise disturbed the Cat, who was asleep on the hearthrug. Looking up at the intruder, she said, "Who may you be, and where have you come from?" The Parrot replied, "Your master has just bought me and brought me home with him." "You impudent bird," said the Cat, "how dare you, a newcomer, make a noise like that? Why, I was born here, and have lived here all my life, and yet, if I venture to mew, they throw things at me and chase me all over the place." "Look here, mistress," said the Parrot, “you just hold your tongue. My voice they delight in; but yours—yours is a perfect nuisance.”

Don’t speak ill of others.

10. The Ass and the Mule

A certain man who had an Ass and a Mule loaded them both up one day and set out upon a journey. So long as the road was fairly level, the Ass got on very well: but by and by they came to a place among the hills where the road was very rough and steep, and the Ass was at his last gasp. So he begged the Mule to relieve him of a part of his load: but the Mule refused. At last, from sheer weariness, the Ass stumbled and fell down a steep place and was killed.

The driver was in despair, but he did the best he could: he added the Ass's load to the Mule's, and he also flayed the Ass and put his skin on the top of the double load. The Mule could only just manage the extra weight, and, as he staggered painfully along, he said to himself, "I have only got what I deserved: if I had been willing to help the Ass at first, I should not now be carrying his load and his skin into the bargain."

Help one another.

11. The Goods and the Ills

There was a time in the youth of the world when Goods and Ills entered equally into the concerns of men, so that the Goods did not prevail to make them altogether blessed, nor the Ills to make them wholly miserable.

But owing to the foolishness of mankind the Ills multiplied greatly in number and increased in strength, until it seemed as though they would deprive the Goods of all share in human affairs, and banish them from the earth.

The latter, therefore, betook themselves to heaven and complained to Jupiter of the treatment they had received, at the same time praying him to grant them protection from the Ills, and to advise them concerning the manner of their intercourse with men.

Jupiter granted their request for protection, and decreed that for the future they should not go among men openly in a body, and so be liable to attack from the hostile Ills, but singly and unobserved, and at infrequent and unexpected intervals.

Hence it is that the earth is full of Ills, for they come and go as they please and are never far away; while Goods, alas! come one by one only, and have to travel all the way from heaven, so that they are very seldom seen.

Vices are their own punishment.

12. The Old Woman and the Wine-Jar

An old Woman picked up an empty Wine-jar which had once contained a rare and costly wine, and which still retained some traces of its exquisite bouquet. She raised it to her nose and sniffed at it again and again. "Ah," she cried, "how delicious must have been the liquid which has left behind so ravishing a smell."

The memory of a good deed lives.

13. The Horse and the Groom

There was once a Groom who used to spend long hours clipping and combing the Horse of which he had charge, but who daily stole a portion of his allowance of oats, and sold it for his own profit. The Horse gradually got into worse and worse condition, and at last cried to the Groom, "If you really want me to look sleek and well, you must comb me less and feed me more."

If you wish to do a service, do it right.

14. The Boy and the Snails

A Farmer's Boy went looking for Snails, and, when he had picked up both his hands full, he set about making a fire at which to roast them; for he meant to eat them. When it got well alight and the Snails began to feel the heat, they gradually withdrew more and more into their shells with the hissing noise they always make when they do so. When the Boy heard it, he said, "You abandoned creatures, how can you find heart to whistle when your houses are burning?"

Inappropriateness is to blame.

15. The Farmer and Fortune

A Farmer was ploughing one day on his farm when he turned up a pot of golden coins with his plough. He was overjoyed at his discovery, and from that time forth made an offering daily at the shrine of the Goddess of the Earth. Fortune was displeased at this, and came to him and said, "My man, why do you give Earth the credit for the gift which I bestowed upon you? You never thought of thanking me for your good luck; but should you be unlucky enough to lose what you have gained I know very well that I, Fortune, should then come in for all the blame."

Show gratitude where gratitude is due.

16. The Mistress and Her Servants

A Widow, thrifty and industrious, had two servants, whom she kept pretty hard at work. They were not allowed to lie long abed in the mornings, but the old lady had them up and doing as soon as the cock crew. They disliked intensely having to get up at such an hour, especially in winter-time: and they thought that if it were not for the cock waking up their Mistress so horribly early, they could sleep longer.

So they caught it and wrung its neck. But they weren't prepared for the consequences. For what happened was that their Mistress, not hearing the cock crow as usual, waked them up earlier than ever, and set them to work in the middle of the night.

Some things you cannot change.

17. The Lamp

A Lamp, well filled with oil, burned with a clear and steady light, and began to swell with pride and boast that it shone more brightly than the sun himself.

Just then a puff of wind came and blew it out. Some one struck a match and lit it again, and said, "You just keep alight, and never mind the sun. Why, even the stars never need to be relit as you had to be just now."

Do not boast lest you be taken down.

18. The Goat and the Vine

A Goat was straying in a vineyard, and began to browse on the tender shoots of a Vine which bore several fine bunches of grapes. "What have I done to you," said the Vine, "that you should harm me thus? Isn't there grass enough for you to feed on? All the same, even if you eat up every leaf I have, and leave me quite bare, I shall produce wine enough to pour over you when you are led to the altar to be sacrificed."

Retribution is certain.

19. The Dolphins, the Whales, and the Sprat

The Dolphins quarrelled with the Whales, and before very long they began fighting with one another. The battle was very fierce, and had lasted some time without any sign of coming to an end, when a Sprat thought that perhaps he could stop it; so he stepped in and tried to persuade them

to give up fighting and make friends. But one of the Dolphins said to him contemptuously, "We would rather go on fighting till we're all killed than be reconciled by a Sprat like you!"

Some would rather fight than not.

20. The Thunny and the Dolphin

A Thunny gave chace to a dolphin; and when he was just ready to seize him, the thunny struck before he was aware, and the dolphin, in the eagerness of his pursuit, ran himself a ground with him. They were both lost; but the thunny kept his eye still upon the dolphin, and observing him when he was just at last gasp: Well, says he, the thought of death is now easy to me, so long as I see my enemy go for company.

There is satisfaction in taking
one's enemy along if one has to die.

21. The Swollen Fox

A hungry Fox found in a hollow tree a quantity of bread and meat, which some shepherds had placed there against their return. Delighted with his find he slipped in through the narrow aperture and greedily devoured it all. But when he tried to get out again he found himself so swollen after his big meal that he could not squeeze through the hole, and fell to whining and groaning over his misfortune.

Another Fox, happening to pass that way, came and asked him what the matter was; and, on learning the state of the case, said, "Well, my friend, I see nothing for it but for you to stay where you are till you shrink to your former size; you'll get out then easily enough."

Don't be greedy.

22. The Fox Who Served a Lion

A Lion had a Fox to attend on him, and whenever they went hunting the Fox found the prey and the Lion fell upon it and killed it, and then they divided it between them in certain proportions.

But the Lion always got a very large share, and the Fox a very small one, which didn't please the latter at all; so he determined to set up on his own account. He began by trying to steal a lamb from a flock of sheep: but the shepherd saw him and set his dogs on him. The hunter was now the hunted, and was very soon caught and despatched by the dogs.

Better servitude with safety than freedom with danger.

23. The Lion and the Boar

One hot and thirsty day in the height of summer a Lion and a Boar came down to a little spring at the same moment to drink. In a trice they were quarrelling as to who should drink first. The quarrel soon became a fight and they attacked one another with the utmost fury.

Presently, stopping for a moment to take breath, they saw some vultures seated on a rock above evidently waiting for one of them to be killed, when they would fly down and feed upon the carcase. The sight sobered them at once, and they made up their quarrel, saying, "We had much better be friends than fight and be eaten by vultures."

Those who strive are often watched by oth-
ers
who will take advantage of their defeat to
benefit themselves.

24. The Bald Man and the Fly

A Fly settled on the head of a Bald Man and bit him. In his eagerness to kill it, he hit himself a smart slap. But the Fly escaped, and said to him in derision, "You tried to kill me for just one little bite; what will you do to yourself now, for the heavy smack you have just given yourself?"

"Oh, for that blow I bear no grudge," he replied, "for I never intended myself any harm; but as for you, you contemptible insect, who live by sucking human blood, I'd have borne a good deal more than that for the satisfaction of dashing the life out of you!"

You will only injure yourself
if you take notice of despicable enemies.

25. The Shipwrecked Man and the Sea

A Shipwrecked Man cast up on the beach fell asleep after his struggle with the waves. When he woke up, he bitterly reproached the Sea for its treachery in enticing men with its smooth and smiling surface, and then, when they were well embarked, turning in fury upon them and sending both ship and sailors to destruction.

The Sea arose in the form of a woman, and replied, "Lay not the blame on me, O sailor, but on the Winds. By nature I am as calm and safe as the land itself: but the Winds fall upon me with their gusts and gales, and lash me into a fury that is not natural to me."

Understand what you are doing before you do it.

26. The Rivers and the Sea

Once upon a time all the Rivers combined to protest against the action of the Sea in making their waters salt. "When we come to you," said they to the Sea, "we are sweet and drinkable: but when once we have mingled with you, our waters become as briny and unpalatable as your own." The Sea replied shortly, "Keep away from me and you'll remain sweet."

Do not blame others.

27. The Two Bags

Every man carries Two Bags about with him, one in front and one behind, and both are packed full of faults. The Bag in front contains his neighbours' faults, the one behind his own. Hence it is that men do not see their own faults, but never fail to see those of others.

Men see other's faults but not their own.

28. The Mule

A Mule had had a long rest and much good feeding. He was feeling very vigorous indeed, and pranced around loftily, holding his head high.

"My father certainly was a full-blooded racer," he said. "I can feel that distinctly."

Next day he was put into harness again and that evening he was very downhearted indeed.

"I was mistaken," he said. "My father was an Ass after all."

Be sure of your pedigree before you boast of it.

29. The Lion and the Ass

A Lion and an Ass agreed to go hunting together. In their search for game the hunters saw a number of Wild Goats run into a cave, and laid plans to catch them. The Ass was to go into the cave and drive the Goats out, while the Lion would stand at the entrance to strike them down.

The plan worked beautifully. The Ass made such a frightful din in the cave, kicking and braying with all his might, that the Goats came running out in a panic of fear, only to fall victim to the Lion.

The Ass came proudly out of the cave.

"Did you see how I made them run?" he said.

"Yes, indeed," answered the Lion, "and

if I had not known you and your kind I should certainly have run, too."

The loud-mouthed boaster does not impress nor frighten those who know him.

30. The Lion, the Mouse, and the Fox

A Lion was lying asleep at the mouth of his den when a Mouse ran over his back and tickled him so that he woke up with a start and began looking about everywhere to see what it was that had disturbed him. A Fox, who was looking on, thought he would have a joke at the expense of the Lion; so he said, “Well, this is the first time I’ve seen a Lion afraid of a Mouse.” “Afraid of a Mouse?” said the Lion testily: “not I! It’s his bad manners I can’t stand.”

Small liberties can be large offenses.

31. The Eagle and the Arrow

An Eagle sat perched on a lofty rock, keeping a sharp look-out for prey. A huntsman, concealed in a cleft of the mountain and on the watch for game, spied him there and shot an Arrow at him. The shaft struck him full in the breast and pierced him through and through. As he lay in the agonies of death, he turned his eyes upon the Arrow. “Ah! cruel fate!” he cried, “that I should perish thus: but oh! fate more cruel still, that the Arrow which kills me should be winged with an Eagle’s feathers!”

The misfortunes arising from a man’s own misconduct are the hardest to bear.

32. The Oak and the Reeds

A Giant Oak stood near a brook in which grew some slender Reeds. When the wind blew, the great Oak stood proudly upright with its hundred arms uplifted to the sky. But the Reeds bowed low in the wind and sang a sad and mournful song.

"You have reason to complain," said the Oak. "The slightest breeze that ruffles the surface of the water makes you bow your heads, while I, the mighty Oak, stand upright and firm before the howling tempest." "Do not worry about us," replied the Reeds. "The winds do not harm us. We bow before them and so we do not break. You, in all your pride and strength, have so far resisted their blows. But the end is coming."

As the Reeds spoke a great hurricane rushed out of the north. The Oak stood proudly and fought against the storm, while the yielding Reeds bowed low. The wind redoubled in fury, and all at once the great tree fell, torn up by the roots, and lay among the pitying Reeds.

Better to yield when it is folly to resist,
than to resist stubbornly and be destroyed.

33. The Viper and the File

A Viper entered a carpenter's shop, and went from one to another of the tools, begging for something to eat. Among the rest, he addressed himself to the File, and asked for the favour of a meal. The File replied in a tone of pitying contempt, "What a simpleton you must be if you imagine you will get anything from me, who invariably take from every one and never give anything in return."

The covetous are poor givers.

34. The Soldier and His Horse

A Soldier gave his Horse a plentiful supply of oats in time of war, and tended him with the utmost care, for he wished him to be strong to endure the hardships of the field, and swift to bear his master, when need arose, out of the reach of danger.

But when the war was over he employed him on all sorts of drudgery, bestowing but little attention upon him, and giving him, moreover, nothing but chaff to eat.

The time came when war broke out again, and the Soldier saddled and bridled his Horse, and, having put on his heavy coat of mail, mounted him to ride off and take the field. But the poor half-starved beast sank down under his weight, and said to his rider,

"You will have to go into battle on foot this time. Thanks to hard work and bad food, you have turned me from a Horse into an ass; and you cannot in a moment turn me back again into a Horse."

Care defines ability.

35. The Clown and the Countryman

A Nobleman announced his intention of giving a public entertainment in the theatre, and offered splendid prizes to all who had any novelty to exhibit at the performance. The announcement attracted a crowd of conjurers, jugglers, and acrobats, and among the rest a Clown, very popular with the crowd, who let it be known that he was going to give an entirely new turn.

When the day of the performance came, the theatre was filled from top to bottom some time before the entertainment began. Several performers exhibited their tricks, and then the popular favourite came on empty-handed and alone.

At once there was a hush of expectation:

and he, letting his head fall upon his breast, imitated the squeak of a pig to such perfection that the audience insisted on his producing the animal, which, they said, he must have somewhere concealed about his person.

He, however, convinced them that there was no pig there, and then the applause was deafening. Among the spectators was a Countryman, who disparaged the Clown's performance and announced that he would give a much superior exhibition of the same trick on the following day.

Again the theatre was filled to overflowing, and again the Clown gave his imitation amidst the cheers of the crowd. The Countryman, meanwhile, before going on the stage, had secreted a young porker under his smock; and when the spectators derisively bade him do better if he could, he gave it a pinch in the ear and made it squeal loudly. But they all with one voice shouted out that the Clown's imitation was much more true to life. Thereupon he produced the pig from under his smock and said sarcastically, "There, that shows what sort of judges you are!"

Critics are not always to be depended upon.

36. The Prophet

A Prophet sat in the market-place and told the fortunes of all who cared to engage his services. Suddenly there came running up one who told him that his house had been broken into by thieves, and that they had made off with everything they could lay hands on. He was up in a moment, and rushed off, tearing his hair and calling down curses on the miscreants. The bystanders were much amused, and one of them said, "Our friend professes to know what is going to happen to others, but it seems he's not clever enough to perceive what's in store for himself."

Look back on your life
before you talk about someone else's life.

37. The Trumpeter Taken Prisoner

A Trumpeter marched into battle in the van of the army and put courage into his comrades by his warlike tunes. Being captured by the enemy, he begged for his life, and said, "Do not put me to death; I have killed no one: indeed, I have no weapons, but carry with me only my trumpet here." But his captors replied, "That is only the more reason why we should take your life; for, though you do not fight yourself, you stir up others to do so."

He who incites strife is as guilty as they who strive.

38. The Hound and the Hare

A young Hound started a Hare, and, when he caught her up, would at one moment snap at her with his teeth as though he were about to kill her, while at another he would let go his hold and frisk about her, as if he were playing with another dog. At last the Hare said, "I wish you would show yourself in your true colours! If you are my

friend, why do you bite me? If you are my enemy, why do you play with me?”

He is no friend who plays double.

39. The Old Hound

A Hound who had served his master well for years, and had run down many a quarry in his time, began to lose his strength and speed owing to age.

One day, when out hunting, his master started a powerful wild boar and set the Hound at him. The latter seized the beast by the ear, but his teeth were gone and he could not retain his hold; so the boar escaped. His master began to scold him severely, but the Hound interrupted him with these words: "My will is as strong as ever, master, but my body is old and feeble. You ought to honour me for what I have been instead of abusing me for what I am."

No one should be blamed for his infirmities.

40. The Eagle, the Cat, and the Wild Sow

An Eagle built her nest at the top of a high tree; a Cat with her family occupied a hollow in the trunk half-way down; and a Wild Sow and her young took up their quarters at the foot. They might have got on very well as neighbours had it not been for the evil cunning of the Cat.

Climbing up to the Eagle's nest she said to the Eagle, "You and I are in the greatest possible danger. That dreadful creature, the Sow, who is always to be seen grubbing away at the foot of the tree, means to uproot it, that she may devour your family and mine at her ease."

Having thus driven the Eagle almost out of her senses with terror, the Cat climbed down the tree, and said to the Sow, "I must warn you against that dreadful bird, the Eagle. She is only waiting her chance to fly down and carry off one of your little pigs when you take them out, to feed her brood with." She succeeded in frightening the Sow as much as the Eagle. Then she returned to her hole in the trunk, from which, feigning to be afraid, she never came forth by day. Only by night did she creep out unseen to procure food for her kittens. The Eagle, meanwhile was afraid to stir from her nest, and the Sow dared not leave her home among the roots: so that in time both they and their families perished of hunger, and their dead bodies supplied the Cat with ample food for her growing family.

Don't let fear paralyze you.

41. Venus and the Cat

A Cat fell in love with a handsome young man, and begged the goddess Venus to change her into a woman. Venus was very gracious about it, and changed her at once into a beautiful maiden, whom the young man fell in love with at first sight and shortly afterwards married.

One day Venus thought she would like to see whether the Cat had changed her habits as well as her form; so she let a mouse run loose in the room where they were. Forgetting everything, the young woman had no sooner seen the mouse than up she jumped and was after it like a shot: at which the goddess was so disgusted that she changed her back again into a Cat.

Nature exceeds nurture.

42. The Goatherd and the Goat

A Goat strayed away from the flock, tempted by a patch of clover. The Goatherd tried to call it back, but in vain. It would not obey him.

Then he picked up a stone and threw it, breaking the Goat's horn. The Goatherd was frightened.

"Do not tell the master," he begged the Goat.

"No," said the Goat, "that broken horn can speak for itself!"

Wicked deeds will not stay hiden.

43. The Blackamoor

A Man once bought an Ethiopian slave, who had a black skin like all Ethiopians; but his new master thought his colour was due to his late owner's having neglected him, and that all he wanted was a good scrubbing.

So he set to work with plenty of soap and hot water, and rubbed away at him with a will, but all to no purpose: his skin remained as black as ever, while the poor wretch all but died from the cold he caught.

What's bred in the bone will stick to the flesh.

44. The Labourer and the Snake

A Labourer's little son was bitten by a Snake and died of the wound. The father was beside himself with grief, and in his anger against the Snake he caught up an axe and went and stood close to the Snake's hole, and watched for a chance of killing it. Presently the Snake came out, and the man aimed a blow at it, but only succeeded in cutting off the tip of its tail before it wriggled in again.

He then tried to get it to come out a second time, pretending that he wished to make up the quarrel. But the Snake said, "I can never be your friend because of my lost tail, nor you mine because of your lost child."

Injuries are never forgotten in the presence of those
who caused them.

45. The Archer and the Lion

An Archer went up into the hills to get some sport with his bow, and all the animals fled at the sight of him with the exception of the Lion, who stayed behind and challenged him to fight. But he shot an arrow at the Lion and hit him, and said, "There, you see what my messenger can do: just you wait a moment and I'll tackle you myself."

The Lion, however, when he felt the sting of the arrow, ran away as fast as his legs could carry him. A fox, who had seen it all happen, said to the Lion, "Come, don't be a coward: why don't you stay and show fight?" But the Lion replied, "You won't get me to stay, not you: why, when he sends a messenger like that before him, he must himself be a terrible fellow to deal with."

Give a wide berth to those who can do damage at a distance.

46. The Debtor and His Sow

A Man of Athens fell into debt and was pressed for the money by his creditor; but he had no means of paying at the time, so he begged for delay. But the creditor refused and said he must pay at once.

Then the Debtor fetched a Sow—the only one he had—and took her to market to offer her for sale. It happened that his creditor was there too. Presently a buyer came along and asked if the Sow produced good litters. "Yes," said the Debtor, "very fine ones; and the remarkable thing is that she produces females at the Mysteries and males at the Panathenea." At that the creditor, who was standing by, put in, "Don't be surprised, sir; why, still better, at the Dionysia this Sow has kids!"

People often swears the impossible for their own merits.

47. The Kingdom of the Lion

When the Lion reigned over the beasts of the earth he was never cruel or tyrannical, but as gentle and just as a King ought to be. During his reign he called a general assembly of the beasts, and drew up a code of laws under which all were to live in perfect equal-

ity and harmony: the wolf and the lamb, the tiger and the stag, the leopard and the kid, the dog and the hare, all should dwell side by side in unbroken peace and friendship. The hare said, “Oh! how I have longed for this day when the weak take their place without fear by the side of the strong!”

Oil and water don’t mix.

48. The Lion, Jupiter, and the Elephant

The Lion, for all his size and strength, and his sharp teeth and claws, is a coward in one thing: he can't bear the sound of a cock crowing, and runs away whenever he hears it.

He complained bitterly to Jupiter for making him like that; but Jupiter said it wasn't his fault: he had done the best he could for him, and, considering this was his only failing, he ought to be well content.

The Lion, however, wouldn't be comforted, and was so ashamed of his timidity that he wished he might die.

In this state of mind, he met the Elephant and had a talk with him. He noticed that the great beast cocked up his ears all the time, as if he were listening for something, and he asked him why he did so.

Just then a gnat came humming by, and the Elephant said, "Do you see that wretched little buzzing insect? I'm terribly afraid of its getting into my ear: if it once gets in, I'm dead and done for."

The Lion's spirits rose at once when he heard this: "For," he said to himself, "if the Elephant, huge as he is, is afraid of a gnat, I needn't be so much ashamed of being afraid of a cock, who is ten thousand times bigger than a gnat."

There is always someone else worse off than you.

49. The Wolves and the Dogs

Once upon a time the Wolves said to the Dogs, “Why should we continue to be enemies any longer? You are very like us in most ways: the main difference between us is one of training only. We live a life of freedom; but you are enslaved to mankind, who beat you, and put heavy collars round your necks, and compel you to keep watch over their flocks and herds for them, and, to crown all, they give you nothing but bones to eat. Don’t put up with it any longer, but hand over the flocks to us, and we will all live on the fat of the land and feast together.” The Dogs allowed themselves to be persuaded by these words, and accompanied the Wolves into their den. But no sooner were they well inside than the Wolves set upon them and tore them to pieces.

Traitors richly deserve their fate.

50. The Fly and the Draught-Mule

A Fly sat on one of the shafts of a cart and said to the Mule who was pulling it, "How slow you are! Do mend your pace, or I shall have to use my sting as a goad." The Mule was not in the least disturbed. "Behind me, in the cart," said he, "sits my master. He holds the reins, and flicks me with his whip, and him I obey, but I don't want any of your impertinence. I know when I may dawdle and when I may not."

Ignore complainers who have no influence.

51. The Pack-Ass and the Wild Ass

A Wild Ass, who was wandering idly about, one day came upon a Pack-Ass lying at full length in a sunny spot and thoroughly enjoying himself. Going up to him, he said, "What a lucky beast you are! Your sleek coat shows how well you live: how I envy you!"

Not long after the Wild Ass saw his acquaintance again, but this time he was carrying a heavy load, and his driver was following behind and beating him with a thick stick. "Ah, my friend," said the Wild Ass, "I don't envy you any more: for I see you pay dear for your comforts."

Advantages that are dearly bought are doubtful blessings.

52. The Pack-Ass, the Wild Ass, and the Lion

A Wild Ass saw a Pack-Ass jogging along under a heavy load, and taunted him with the condition of slavery in which he lived, in these words: "What a vile lot is yours compared with mine! I am free as the air, and never do a stroke of work; and, as for fodder, I have only to go to the hills and there I find far more than enough for my needs. But you! you depend on your master for food, and he makes you carry heavy loads every day and beats you unmercifully."

At that moment a Lion appeared on the scene, and made no attempt to molest the Pack-Ass owing to the presence of the driver; but he fell upon the Wild Ass, who had no one to protect him, and without more ado made a meal of him.

It is no use being your own master
unless you can stand up for yourself.

53. The Ass in the Lion's Skin

An Ass found a Lion's skin left in the forest by a hunter. He dressed himself in it, and amused himself by hiding in a thicket and rushing out suddenly at the animals who passed that way. All took to their heels the moment they saw him.

The Ass was so pleased to see the animals running away from him, just as if he were King Lion himself, that he could not keep from expressing his delight by a loud, harsh bray. A Fox, who ran with the rest, stopped short as soon as he heard the voice. Approaching the Ass, he said with a laugh: "If you had kept your mouth shut you might have frightened me, too. But you gave yourself away with that silly bray."

A fool may deceive by his dress and appearance,
but his words will soon show what he really is.

54. The Ant

Ants were once men and made their living by tilling the soil. But, not content with the results of their own work, they were always casting longing eyes upon the crops and fruits of their neighbours, which they stole, whenever they got the chance, and added to their own store.

At last their covetousness made Jupiter so angry that he changed them into Ants. But, though their forms were changed, their nature remained the same: and so, to this day, they go about among the cornfields and gather the fruits of others' labour, and store them up for their own use.

You may punish a thief, but his bent remains.

55. The Ass and His Purchaser

A Man who wanted to buy an Ass went to market, and, coming across a likely-looking beast, arranged with the owner that he should be allowed to take him home on trial to see what he was like. When he reached home, he put him into his stable along with the other asses.

The newcomer took a look round, and immediately went and chose a place next to the laziest and greediest beast in the stable. When the master saw this he put a halter on him at once, and led him off and handed him over to his owner again. The latter was a good deal surprised to see him back so soon, and said, "Why, do you mean to say you have tested him already?"

"I don't want to put him through any more tests," replied the other: "I could see what sort of beast he is from the companion he chose for himself."

A man is known by the company he keeps.

56. The Butcher and His Customers

Two Men were buying meat at a Butcher's stall in the market-place, and, while the Butcher's back was turned for a moment, one of them snatched up a joint and hastily thrust it under the other's cloak, where it could not be seen.

When the Butcher turned round, he missed the meat at once, and charged them with having stolen it: but the one who had taken it said he hadn't got it, and the one who had got it said he hadn't taken it. The Butcher felt sure they were deceiving him, but he only said, "You may cheat me with your lying, but you can't cheat the gods, and they won't let you off so lightly."

Prevarication often amounts to perjury.

57. The Bald Huntsman

A Man who had lost all his hair took to wearing a wig, and one day he went out hunting. It was blowing rather hard at the time, and he hadn't gone far before a gust of wind caught his hat and carried it off, and his wig too, much to the amusement of the hunt. But he quite entered into the joke, and said, "Ah, well! the hair that wig is made of didn't stick to the head on which it grew; so it's no wonder it won't stick to mine."

You can't own something that's not supposed to be yours.

58. The Father and His Daughters

A Man had two Daughters, one of whom he gave in marriage to a gardener, and the other to a potter. After a time he thought he would go and see how they were getting on; and first he went to the gardener's wife. He asked her how she was, and how things were going with herself and her husband.

She replied that on the whole they were doing very well: "But," she continued, "I do wish we could have some good heavy rain: the garden wants it badly." Then he went on to the potter's wife and made the same inquiries of her. She replied that she and her husband had nothing to complain of: "But," she went on, "I do wish we could have some nice dry weather, to dry the pottery."

Her Father looked at her with a humorous expression on his face. "You want dry weather," he said, "and your sister wants rain. I was going to ask in my prayers that your wishes should be granted; but now it strikes me I had better not refer to the subject."

You can't please everyone.

59. The Three Tradesmen

The citizens of a certain city were debating about the best material to use in the fortifications which were about to be erected for the greater security of the town. A Carpenter got up and advised the use of wood, which he said was readily procurable and easily worked. A Stone-mason objected to wood on the ground that it was so inflammable, and recommended stones instead. Then a Tanner got on his legs and said, "In my opinion there's nothing like leather."

Every man for himself.

60. The Thief and the Innkeeper

A Thief hired a room at an inn, and stayed there some days on the look-out for something to steal.

No opportunity, however, presented itself, till one day, when there was a festival to be celebrated, the Innkeeper appeared in a fine new coat and sat down before the door of the inn for an airing. The Thief no sooner set eyes upon the coat than he longed to get possession of it. There was no business doing, so he went and took a seat by the side of the Innkeeper, and began talking to him. They conversed together for some time, and then the Thief suddenly yawned and howled like a wolf. The Innkeeper asked him in some concern what ailed him. The

Thief replied, "I will tell you about myself, sir, but first I must beg you to take charge of my clothes for me, for I intend to leave them with you. Why I have these fits of yawning I cannot tell: maybe they are sent as a punishment for my misdeeds; but, whatever the reason, the facts are that when I have yawned three times I become a ravening wolf and fly at men's throats."

As he finished speaking he yawned a second time and howled again as before. The Innkeeper, believing every word he said, and terrified at the prospect of being confronted with a wolf, got up hastily and started to run indoors; but the Thief caught him by the coat and tried to stop him, crying, "Stay, sir, stay, and take charge of my clothes, or else I shall never see them again."

As he spoke he opened his mouth and began to yawn for the third time. The Innkeeper, mad with the fear of being eaten by a wolf, slipped out of his coat, which remained in the other's hands, and bolted into the inn and locked the door behind him; and the Thief then quietly stole off with his spoil.

Every tale is not to be believed.

61. Hercules and Minerva

Hercules was once travelling along a narrow road when he saw lying on the ground in front of him what appeared to be an apple, and as he passed he stamped upon it with his heel. To his astonishment, instead of being crushed it doubled in size; and, on his attacking it again and smiting it with his club, it swelled up to an enormous size and blocked up the whole road.

Upon this he dropped his club, and stood looking at it in amazement. Just then Minerva appeared, and said to him, "Leave it alone, my friend; that which you see before you is the apple of discord: if you do not meddle with it, it remains small as it was at first, but if you resort to violence it swells into the thing you see."

Fight brings greater damage.

62. The Frogs Who Wished for a King

The Frogs were tired of governing themselves. They had so much freedom that it had spoiled them, and they did nothing but sit around croaking in a bored manner and wishing for a government that could entertain them with the pomp and display of royalty, and rule them in a way to make them know they were being ruled. No milk and water government for them, they declared. So they sent a petition to Jupiter asking for a king.

Jupiter saw what simple and foolish creatures they were, but to keep them quiet and make them think they had a king he threw down a huge log, which fell into the water with a great splash. The Frogs hid themselves among the reeds and grasses,

thinking the new king to be some fearful giant. But they soon discovered how tame and peaceable King Log was. In a short time the younger Frogs were using him for a diving platform, while the older Frogs made him a meeting place, where they complained loudly to Jupiter about the government.

To teach the Frogs a lesson the ruler of the gods now sent a Crane to be king of

Frogland. The Crane proved to be a very different sort of king from old King Log. He gobbled up the poor Frogs right and left and they soon saw what fools they had been. In mournful croaks they begged Jupiter to take away the cruel tyrant before they should all be destroyed.

"How now!" cried Jupiter "Are you not yet content? You have what you asked for and so you have only yourselves to blame for your misfortunes."

Be sure you can better your condition before you seek to change.

63. The Crow and the Snake

A hungry Crow spied a Snake lying asleep in a sunny spot, and, picking it up in his claws, he was carrying it off to a place where he could make a meal of it without being disturbed, when the Snake reared its head and bit him. It was a poisonous Snake, and the bite was fatal, and the dying Crow said, “What a cruel fate is mine! I thought I had made a lucky find, and it has cost me my life!”

Desire things you don’t understand and you accept the consequences.

64. The Eagle and the Fox

An Eagle and a Fox became great friends and determined to live near one another: they thought that the more they saw of each other the better friends they would be. So the Eagle built a nest at the top of a high tree, while the Fox settled in a thicket at the foot of it and produced a litter of cubs.

One day the Fox went out foraging for food, and the Eagle, who also wanted food for her young, flew down into the thicket, caught up the Fox's cubs, and carried them up into the tree for a meal for herself and her family.

When the Fox came back, and found out what had happened, she was not so much sorry for the loss of her cubs as furious because she couldn't get at the Eagle and pay her out for her treachery.

So she sat down not far off and cursed her. But it wasn't long before she had her revenge.

Some villagers happened to be sacrificing a goat on a neighbouring altar, and the Eagle flew down and carried off a piece of burning flesh to her nest. There was a strong wind blowing, and the nest caught fire, with the result that her fledglings fell half-roasted to the ground.

Then the Fox ran to the spot and devoured them in full sight of the Eagle.

False faith may escape human punishment,
but cannot escape the divine.

65. The Fox and the Bramble

In making his way through a hedge a Fox missed his footing and caught at a Bramble to save himself from falling. Naturally, he got badly scratched, and in disgust he cried to the Bramble, "It was your help I wanted, and see how you have treated me! I'd sooner have fallen outright."

The Bramble, interrupting him, replied, "You must have lost your wits, my friend, to catch at me, who am myself always catching at others."

Sometimes you have to ask your enemies for help.

66. The Horse and the Stag

There was once a Horse who used to graze in a meadow which he had all to himself. But one day a Stag came into the meadow, and said he had as good a right to feed there as the Horse, and moreover chose all the best places for himself. The Horse, wishing to be revenged upon his unwelcome visitor, went to a man and asked if he would help him to turn out the Stag. "Yes," said the man, "I will by all means; but I can only do so if you let me put a bridle in your mouth and mount on your back."

The Horse agreed to this, and the two together very soon turned the Stag out of the pasture: but when that was done, the Horse found to his dismay that in the man he had got a master for good.

He who seeks to injure others often injures only himself.

67. The Thieves and the Cock

Some Thieves broke into a house, and found nothing worth taking except a Cock, which they seized and carried off with them.

When they were preparing their supper, one of them caught up the Cock, and was about to wring his neck, when he cried out

for mercy and said, "Pray do not kill me: you will find me a most useful bird, for I rouse honest men to their work in the morning by my crowing." But the Thief replied with some heat, "Yes, I know you do, making it still harder for us to get a livelihood. Into the pot you go!"

The safeguards of virtue are hateful to those with evil intentions.

68. The Shepherd and the Wolf

A Shepherd found a Wolf's Cub straying in the pastures, and took him home and reared him along with his dogs. When the Cub grew to his full size, if ever a wolf stole a sheep from the flock, he used to join the dogs in hunting him down. It sometimes happened that the dogs failed to come up with the thief, and, abandoning the pursuit, returned home. The Wolf would on such occasions continue the chase by himself, and when he overtook the culprit, would stop and share the feast with him, and then return to the Shepherd.

But if some time passed without a sheep being carried off by the wolves, he would steal one himself and share his plunder with the dogs. The Shepherd's suspicions were aroused, and one day he caught him in the act; and, fastening a rope round his neck, hung him on the nearest tree.

What's bred in the bone is sure to come out in the flesh.

69. The Gardener and His Dog

A Gardner's Dog fell into a deep well, from which his master used to draw water for the plants in his garden with a rope and a bucket. Failing to get the Dog out by means of these, the Gardener went down into the well himself in order to fetch him up.

But the Dog thought he had come to make sure of drowning him; so he bit his master as soon as he came within reach, and hurt him a good deal, with the result that he left the Dog to his fate and climbed out of the well, remarking, "It serves me quite right for trying to save so determined a suicide."

Benefits are refused by those who don't understand them.

70. The Fowler and the Lark

A Fowler was setting his nets for little birds when a Lark came up to him and asked him what he was doing. "I am engaged in founding a city," said he, and with that he withdrew to a short distance and concealed himself.

The Lark examined the nets with great curiosity, and presently, catching sight of the bait, hopped on to them in order to secure it, and became entangled in the meshes. The Fowler then ran up quickly and captured her. "What a fool I was!" said she: "but at any rate, if that's the kind of city you are founding, it'll be a long time before you find fools enough to fill it."

There is no glory in tricking those easy to trick.

71. The Hunter and the Woodman

A Hunter was searching in the forest for the tracks of a lion, and, catching sight presently of a Woodman engaged in felling a tree, he went up to him and asked him if he had noticed a lion's footprints anywhere about, or if he knew where his den was. The Woodman answered, "If you will come with me, I will show you the lion himself."

The Hunter turned pale with fear, and his teeth chattered as he replied, "Oh, I'm not looking for the lion, thanks, but only for his tracks."

The hero is brave in deeds as well as words.

72. Brother and Sister

A certain man had two children, a boy and a girl: and the boy was as good-looking as the girl was plain. One day, as they were playing together in their mother's chamber, they chanced upon a mirror and saw their own features for the first time. The boy saw what a handsome fellow he was, and began to boast to his Sister about his good looks: she, on her part, was ready to cry with vexation when she was aware of her plainness, and took his remarks as an insult to herself.

Running to her father, she told him of her Brother's conceit, and accused him of meddling with his mother's things. He laughed and kissed them both, and said, "My children, learn from now onwards to make a good use of the glass. You, my boy, strive to be as good as it shows you to be handsome; and you, my girl, resolve to make up for the plainness of your features by the sweetness of your disposition."

Inner beauty is better than outer beauty.

73. Hercules and Plutus

When Hercules was received among the gods and was entertained at a banquet by Jupiter, he responded courteously to the greetings of all with the exception of Plutus, the god of wealth. When Plutus approached him, he cast his eyes upon the ground, and turned away and pretended not to see him.

Jupiter was surprised at this conduct on his part, and asked why, after having been so cordial with all the other gods, he had behaved like that to Plutus. "Sire," said Hercules, "I do not like Plutus, and I will tell you why. When we were on earth together I always noticed that he was to be found in the company of scoundrels."

Even if you're rich, you shouldn't keep your vile nature.

74. The Witch

A Witch professed to be able to avert the anger of the gods by means of charms, of which she alone possessed the secret; and she drove a brisk trade, and made a fat livelihood out of it.

But certain persons accused her of black magic and carried her before the judges, and demanded that she should be put to death for dealings with the Devil. She was found guilty and condemned to death: and one of the judges said to her as she was leaving the dock, "You say you can avert the anger of the gods. How comes it, then, that you have failed to disarm the enmity of men?"

Promise of the great without doing ordinary things,
creates problems.

75. The Sick Man and the Doctor

A Sick Man received a visit from his Doctor, who asked him how he was. "Fairly well, Doctor," said he, "but I find I sweat a great deal."

"Ah," said the Doctor, "that's a good sign."

On his next visit he asked the same question, and his patient replied, "I'm much as usual, but I've taken to having shivering fits, which leave me cold all over."

"Ah," said the Doctor, "that's a good sign too."

When he came the third time and inquired as before about his patient's health, the Sick Man said that he felt very feverish. "A very good sign," said the Doctor; "you are doing very nicely indeed."

Afterwards a friend came to see the invalid, and on asking him how he did, received this reply: "My dear friend, I'm dying of good signs."

A death-bed flattery is the worst of treacheries.

76. The Old Man and Death

An Old Man cut himself a bundle of faggots in a wood and started to carry them home. He had a long way to go, and was tired out before he had got much more than half-way. Casting his burden on the ground, he called upon Death to come and release him from his life of toil.

The words were scarcely out of his mouth when, much to his dismay, Death stood before him and professed his readiness to serve him. He was almost frightened out of his wits, but he had enough presence of mind to stammer out, "Good sir, if you'd be so kind, pray help me up with my burden again."

Be careful what you wish for.

77. The Moon and Her Mother

The Moon once begged her Mother to make her a gown. "How can I?" replied she; "there's no fitting your figure. At one time you're a New Moon, and at another you're a Full Moon; and between whiles you're neither one nor the other."

You have to be consistent and single-minded to achieve your goals.

78. The Rogue and the Oracle

A Rogue laid a wager that he would prove the Oracle at Delphi to be untrustworthy by procuring from it a false reply to an inquiry by himself. So he went to the temple on the appointed day with a small bird in his hand, which he concealed under the folds of his cloak, and asked whether what he held in his hand were alive or dead.

If the Oracle said "dead," he meant to produce the bird alive: if the reply was "alive," he intended to wring its neck and show it to be dead. But the Oracle was one too many for him, for the answer he got was this: "Stranger, whether the thing that you hold in your hand be alive or dead is a matter that depends entirely on your own will."

The Will is the most important thing.

79. The She-Goats and Their Beards

Jupiter granted beards to the She-Goats at their own request, much to the disgust of the he-Goats, who considered this to be an unwarrantable invasion of their rights and dignities. So they sent a deputation to him to protest against his action. He, however, advised them not to raise any objections.

"What's in a tuft of hair?" said he. "Let them have it if they want it. They can never be a match for you in strength."

It matters little if those who are inferior to us in merit
should be like us in outside appearances.

80. The Wolf and the Horse

A Wolf on his rambles came to a field of oats, but, not being able to eat them, he was passing on his way when a Horse came along. "Look," said the Wolf, "here's a fine field of oats. For your sake I have left it untouched, and I shall greatly enjoy the sound of your teeth munching the ripe grain."

But the Horse replied, "If wolves could eat oats, my fine friend, you would hardly have indulged your ears at the cost of your belly."

There is no virtue in giving to others what is useless to oneself.

81. The Wily Lion

A Lion watched a fat Bull feeding in a meadow, and his mouth watered when he thought of the royal feast he would make, but he did not dare to attack him, for he was afraid of his sharp horns. Hunger, however, presently compelled him to do something: and as the use of force did not promise success, he determined to resort to artifice. Going up to the Bull in friendly fashion, he said to him, "I cannot help saying how much I admire your magnificent figure. What a fine head! What powerful shoulders and thighs! But, my dear friend, what in the world makes you wear those ugly horns? You must find them as awkward as they are unsightly. Believe me, you would do much better without them."

The Bull was foolish enough to be persuaded by this flattery to have his horns cut off; and, having now lost his only means of defence, fell an easy prey to the Lion.

When a man has both an interest and an
inclination to betray us,
there's no trusting him.

82. The Frogs Complaint Against the Sun

Once upon a time the Sun was about to take to himself a wife. The Frogs in terror all raised their voices to the skies, and Jupiter, disturbed by the noise, asked them what they were croaking about. They replied, "The Sun is bad enough even while he is single, drying up our marshes with his heat as he does. But what will become of us if he marries and begets other Suns?"

Watch the actions of your enemy.

83. The Wolves, the Sheep, and the Ram

The Wolves sent a deputation to the Sheep with proposals for a lasting peace between them, on condition of their giving up the sheep-dogs to instant death. The foolish Sheep agreed to the terms; but an old Ram, whose years had brought him wisdom, interfered and said, "How can we expect to live at peace with you? Why, even with the dogs at hand to protect us, we are never secure from your murderous attacks!"

A foolish peace is more destructive than a bloody war.

84. The Bull and the Calf

A full-grown Bull was struggling to force his huge bulk through the narrow entrance to a cow-house where his stall was, when a young Calf came up and said to him, "If you'll step aside a moment, I'll show you the way to get through." The Bull turned upon him an amused look. "I knew that way," said he, "before you were born."

Do not presume to teach your elders.

85. The Fox and the Monkey

A Fox and a Monkey were on the road together, and fell into a dispute as to which of the two was the better born. They kept it up for some time, till they came to a place where the road passed through a cemetery full of monuments, when the Monkey stopped and looked about him and gave a great sigh. "Why do you sigh?" said the Fox.

The Monkey pointed to the tombs and replied, "All the monuments that you see here were put up in honour of my forefathers, who in their day were eminent men." The Fox was speechless for a moment, but quickly recovering he said, "Oh! don't stop at any lie, sir; you're quite safe: I'm sure none of your ancestors will rise up and expose you."

Boasters brag most when they cannot be detected.

86. The Bat, the Bramble, and the Seagull

A Bat, a Bramble, and a Seagull went into partnership and determined to go on a trading voyage together. The Bat borrowed a sum of money for his venture; the Bramble laid in a stock of clothes of various kinds; and the Seagull took a quantity of lead: and so they set out.

By and by a great storm came on, and their boat with all the cargo went to the bottom, but the three travellers managed to reach land.

Ever since then the Seagull flies to and fro over the sea, and every now and then dives below the surface, looking for the lead he's lost; while the Bat is so afraid of meeting his creditors that he hides away by day and only comes out at night to feed; and the Bramble catches hold of the clothes of every one who passes by, hoping some day to recognise and recover the lost garments.

All men are more concerned to recover what they lose than to acquire what they lack.

87. The Ploughman, the Ass, and the Ox

A Ploughman yoked his Ox and his Ass together, and set to work to plough his field. It was a poor makeshift of a team, but it was the best he could do, as he had but a single Ox. At the end of the day, when the beasts were loosed from the yoke, the Ass said to the Ox, "Well, we've had a hard day: which of us is to carry the master home?" The Ox looked surprised at the question. "Why," said he, "you, to be sure, as usual."

However lost, don't forget your true work.

88. Demades and His Fable

Demades the orator was once speaking in the Assembly at Athens; but the people were very inattentive to what he was saying, so he stopped and said, "Gentlemen, I should like to tell you one of Aesop's fables." This made every one listen intently. Then Demades began: "Demeter, a Swallow, and an Eel were once travelling together, and came to a river without a bridge: the Swallow flew over it, and the Eel swam across"; and then he stopped. "What happened to Demeter?" cried several people in the audience. "Demeter," he replied, "is very angry with you for listening to fables when you ought to be minding public business."

Don't just do the playful. Do something important.

89. The Fisherman Piping

A Fisherman who could play the flute went down one day to the sea-shore with his nets and his flute; and, taking his stand on a projecting rock, began to play a tune, thinking that the music would bring the fish jumping out of the sea.

He went on playing for some time, but not a fish appeared: so at last he threw down his flute and cast his net into the sea, and made a great haul of fish. When they were landed and he saw them leaping about on the shore, he cried, "You rascals! you wouldn't dance when I piped: but now I've stopped, you can do nothing else!"

Stick to business you know.

90. The Nightingale and the Hawk

A Nightingale was sitting on a bough of an oak and singing, as her custom was. A hungry Hawk presently spied her, and darting to the spot seized her in his talons. He was just about to tear her in pieces when she begged him to spare her life: "I'm not big enough," she pleaded, "to make you a good meal: you ought to seek your prey among the bigger birds." The Hawk eyed her with some contempt. "You must think me very simple," said he, "if you suppose I am going to give up a certain prize on the chance of a better of which I see at present no signs."

A bird in the hand is worth two in the bush.

91. The Rose and the Amaranth

A Rose and an Amaranth blossomed side by side in a garden, and the Amaranth said to her neighbour, "How I envy you your beauty and your sweet scent! No wonder you are such a universal favourite."

But the Rose replied with a shade of sadness in her voice, "Ah, my dear friend, I bloom but for a time: my petals soon wither and fall, and then I die. But your flowers never fade, even if they are cut; for they are everlasting."

Accept your own fate.

92. The Ploughman and the Wolf

A Ploughman loosed his oxen from the plough, and led them away to the water to drink. While he was absent a half-starved Wolf appeared on the scene, and went up to the plough and began chewing the leather straps attached to the yoke.

As he gnawed away desperately in the hope of satisfying his craving for food, he somehow got entangled in the harness, and, taking fright, struggled to get free, tugging at the traces as if he would drag the plough along with him.

Just then the Ploughman came back, and seeing what was happening, he cried, "Ah, you old rascal, I wish you would give up thieving for good and take to honest work instead."

Wicked person cannot gain trust
by doing good deeds occasionally.

93. The Fowler and the Partridge

A Fowler caught a Partridge in his nets, and was just about to wring its neck when it made a piteous appeal to him to spare its life and said, "Do not kill me, but let me live and I will repay you for your kindness by decoying other partridges into your nets."

"No," said the Fowler, "I will not spare you. I was going to kill you anyhow, and after that treacherous speech you thoroughly deserve your fate."

Those who would sacrifice their friends to
save
themselves are not entitled to mercy.

94. The Fowler, the Partridge, and the Cock

One day, as a Fowler was sitting down to a scanty supper of herbs and bread, a friend dropped in unexpectedly. The larder was empty; so he went out and caught a tame Partridge, which he kept as a decoy, and was about to wring her neck when she cried, "Surely you won't kill me? Why, what will you do without me next time you go fowling? How will you get the birds to come to your nets?"

He let her go at this, and went to his hen-house, where he had a plump young Cock. When the Cock saw what he was after, he too pleaded for his life, and said, "If you kill me, how will you know the time of night? and who will wake you up in the morning when it is time to get to work?"

The Fowler, however, replied, "You are useful for telling the time, I know; but, for all that, I can't send my friend supperless to bed." And therewith he caught him and wrung his neck.

Necessity knows no law.

95. The Sheep, the Wolf, and the Stag

One day a Stag came to a Sheep and asked her to lend him a measure of wheat. The Sheep knew him for a very swift runner, who could easily take himself out of reach, were he so inclined. So she asked him if he knew someone who would answer for him.

"Yes, yes," answered the Stag confidently, "the Wolf has promised to be my surety."

"The Wolf!" exclaimed the Sheep indignantly. "Do you think I would trust you on such security? I know the Wolf! He takes what he wants and runs off with it without paying. As for you, you can use your legs so well that I should have little chance of collecting the debt if I had to catch you for it!"

Two blacks do not make a white.

96. The Hawk, the Kite, and the Pigeons

The Pigeons in a certain dovecote were persecuted by a Kite, who every now and then swooped down and carried off one of their number. So they invited a Hawk into the dovecote to defend them against their enemy.

But they soon repented of their folly: for the Hawk killed more of them in a day than the Kite had done in a year.

Avoid a remedy that is worse than the disease.

97. The Swallow and the Crow

A Swallow was once boasting to a Crow about her birth. "I was once a princess," said she, "the daughter of a King of Athens, but my husband used me cruelly, and cut out my tongue for a slight fault. Then, to protect me from further injury, I was turned by Juno into a bird."

"You chatter quite enough as it is," said the Crow. "What you would have been like if you hadn't lost your tongue, I can't think."

Fine weather friends are not worth much.

98. The Hound and the Fox

A Hound, roaming in the forest, spied a lion, and being well used to lesser game, gave chase, thinking he would make a fine quarry.

Presently the lion perceived that he was being pursued; so, stopping short, he rounded on his pursuer and gave a loud roar. The Hound immediately turned tail and fled. A Fox, seeing him running away, jeered at him and said, "Ho! ho! There goes the coward who chased a lion and ran away the moment he roared!"

Don't fight something you can't fight.

99. The Mice and the Weasels

The Weasels and the Mice were always up in arms against each other. In every battle the Weasels carried off the victory, as well as a large number of the Mice, which they ate for dinner next day. In despair the Mice called a council, and there it was decided that the Mouse army was always beaten because it had no leaders. So a large number of generals and commanders were appointed from among the most eminent Mice.

To distinguish themselves from the soldiers in the ranks, the new leaders proudly bound on their heads lofty crests and ornaments of feathers or straw.

Then after long preparation of the Mouse army in all the arts of war, they sent a challenge to the Weasels.

The Weasels accepted the challenge with eagerness, for they were always ready for a fight when a meal was in sight.

They immediately attacked the Mouse army in large numbers. Soon the Mouse line gave way before the attack and the whole army fled for cover.

The privates easily slipped into their holes, but the Mouse leaders could not squeeze through the narrow openings because of their head-dresses. Not one escaped the teeth of the hungry Weasels.

Greatness has its penalties.

100. The Lion and the Gnat

"Away with you, vile insect!" said a Lion angrily to a Gnat that was buzzing around his head. But the Gnat was not in the least disturbed.

"Do you think," he said spitefully to the Lion, "that I am afraid of you because they call you king?"

The next instant he flew at the Lion and stung him sharply on the nose. Mad with rage, the Lion struck fiercely at the Gnat, but only succeeded in tearing himself with his claws. Again and again the Gnat stung the Lion, who now was roaring terribly. At last, worn out with rage and covered with wounds that his own teeth and claws had made, the Lion gave up the fight.

The Gnat buzzed away to tell the whole world about his victory, but instead he flew straight into a spider's web. And there, he who had defeated the King of beasts came to a miserable end, the prey of a little spider.

The least of our enemies is often the most to be feared.

Pride over a success should not throw us off our guard.

101. The Wolf and the Shepherd

A Wolf, lurking near the Shepherd's hut, saw the Shepherd and his family feasting on a roasted lamb.

"Aha!" he muttered. "What a great shouting and running about there would have been, had they caught me at just the very thing they are doing with so much enjoyment!"

Men often condemn others for what they see
no wrong
in doing themselves.

102. The Hunter and the Horseman

A Hunter went out after game, and succeeded in catching a hare, which he was carrying home with him when he met a man on horseback, who said to him, "You have had some sport I see, sir," and offered to buy it. The Hunter readily agreed; but the Horseman had no sooner got the hare in his hands than he set spurs to his horse and went off at full gallop.

The Hunter ran after him for some little distance; but it soon dawned upon him that he had been tricked, and he gave up trying to overtake the Horseman, and, to save his face, called after him as loud as he could, "All right, sir, all right, take your hare: it was meant all along as a present."

A fool will make excuses for foolish behavior.

103. The Belly and the Members

The Members of the Body once rebelled against the Belly. "You," they said to the Belly, "live in luxury and sloth, and never do a stroke of work; while we not only have to do all the hard work there is to be done, but are actually your slaves and have to minister to all your wants. Now, we will do so no longer, and you can shift for yourself for the future."

They were as good as their word, and left the Belly to starve. The result was just what might have been expected: the whole Body soon began to fail, and the Members and all shared in the general collapse. And then they saw too late how foolish they had been.

The person who withdraws support for his leader is a traitor.

104. The Flea and the Man

A Flea bit a Man, and bit him again, and again, till he could stand it no longer, but made a thorough search for it, and at last succeeded in catching it. Holding it between his finger and thumb, he said—or rather shouted, so angry was he—"Who are you, pray, you wretched little creature, that you make so free with my person?" The Flea, terrified, whimpered in a weak little voice, "Oh, sir! pray let me go; don't kill me! I am such a little thing that I can't do you much harm."

But the Man laughed and said, "I am going to kill you now, at once: whatever is bad has got to be destroyed, no matter how slight the harm it does."

Do not waste your pity on a scamp.

105. The Image-Seller

A certain man made a wooden Image of Mercury, and exposed it for sale in the market. As no one offered to buy it, however, he thought he would try to attract a purchaser by proclaiming the virtues of the Image. So he cried up and down the market, "A god for sale! a god for sale! One who'll bring you luck and keep you lucky!" Presently one of the bystanders stopped him and said, "If your god is all you make him out to be, how is it you don't keep him and make the most of him yourself?" "I'll tell you why," replied he; "he brings gain, it is true, but he takes his time about it; whereas I want money at once."

When you lie, you often have to expand the lie.

106. The Old Woman and the Doctor

An Old Woman became almost totally blind from a disease of the eyes, and, after consulting a Doctor, made an agreement with him in the presence of witnesses that she should pay him a high fee if he cured her, while if he failed he was to receive nothing.

The Doctor accordingly prescribed a course of treatment, and every time he paid her a visit he took away with him some article out of the house, until at last, when he visited her for the last time, and the cure was complete, there was nothing left.

When the Old Woman saw that the house was empty she refused to pay him his fee; and, after repeated refusals on her part, he sued her before the magistrates for payment of her debt. On being brought into court she was ready with her defence.

"The claimant," said she, "has stated the facts about our agreement correctly. I undertook to pay him a fee if he cured me, and he, on his part, promised to charge nothing if he failed. Now, he says I am cured; but I say that I am blinder than ever, and I can prove what I say. When my eyes were bad I could at any rate see well enough to be aware that my house contained a certain amount of furniture and other things; but now, when according to him I am cured, I am entirely unable to see anything there at all."

Few things are done except for profit.

107. The Woman and Her Hen

A woman possessed a Hen that gave her an egg every day. She often thought with herself how she might obtain two eggs daily instead of one, and at last, to gain her purpose, determined to give the Hen a double allowance of barley. From that day the Hen became fat and sleek, and never once laid another egg.

Covetousness overreacheth itself.

108. The Weasel and the Man

A Man once caught a Weasel, which was always sneaking about the house, and was just going to drown it in a tub of water, when it begged hard for its life, and said to him, "Surely you haven't the heart to put me to death? Think how useful I have been in clearing your house of the mice and lizards which used to infest it, and show your gratitude by sparing my life."

"You have not been altogether useless, I grant you," said the Man: "but who killed the fowls? Who stole the meat? No, no! You do much more harm than good, and die you shall."

It is sometimes wise to turn circumstances.

109. The Charger and the Miller

A Horse, who had been used to carry his rider into battle, felt himself growing old and chose to work in a mill instead. He now no longer found himself stepping out proudly to the beating of the drums, but was compelled to slave away all day grinding the corn. Bewailing his hard lot, he said one day to the Miller, "Ah me! I was once a splendid war-horse, gaily caparisoned, and attended by a groom whose sole duty was to see to my wants. How different is my present condition! I wish I had never given up the battle-field for the mill."

The Miller replied with asperity, "It's no use your regretting the past. Fortune has many ups and downs: you must just take them as they come."

Fortune has its ups and downs.

110. The Ass and the Old Peasant

An old Peasant was sitting in a meadow watching his Ass, which was grazing close by, when all of a sudden he caught sight of armed men stealthily approaching. He jumped up in a moment, and begged the Ass to fly with him as fast as he could, "Or else," said he, "we shall both be captured by the enemy." But the Ass just looked round lazily and said, "And if so, do you think they'll make me carry heavier loads than I have to now?" "No," said his master. "Oh, well, then," said the Ass, "I don't mind if they do take me, for I shan't be any worse off."

In a change of government the poor change nothing beyond the name of their master.

111. The Horse and the Ass

A Horse, proud of his fine harness, met an Ass on the high-road. As the Ass with his heavy burden moved slowly out of the way to let him pass, the Horse cried out im-

patiently that he could hardly resist kicking him to make him move faster. The Ass held his peace, but did not forget the other's insolence. Not long afterwards the Horse became broken-winded, and was sold by his owner to a farmer.

One day, as he was drawing a dung-cart, he met the Ass again, who in turn derided him and said, "Aha! you never thought to come to this, did you, you who were so proud! Where are all your gay trappings now?"

Without charity in the present,
don't expect charity in the future.

112. The Thirsty Pigeon

A Pigeon, oppressed by excessive thirst, saw a goblet of water painted on a signboard. Not supposing it to be only a picture, she flew towards it with a loud whir and unwittingly dashed against the signboard, jarring herself terribly. Having broken her wings by the blow, she fell to the ground, and was caught by one of the bystanders.

Act in haste and repent at leisure.

113. The Escaped Jackdaw

A Man caught a Jackdaw and tied a piece of string to one of its legs, and then gave it to his children for a pet. But the Jackdaw didn't at all like having to live with people; so, after a while, when he seemed to have become fairly tame and they didn't watch him so closely, he slipped away and flew back to his old haunts.

Unfortunately, the string was still on his leg, and before long it got entangled in the branches of a tree and the Jackdaw couldn't get free, try as he would. He saw it was all up with him, and cried in despair, "Alas, in gaining my freedom I have lost my life."

Get something small and lose something big.

114. The Two Frogs

Two Frogs were neighbours. One lived in a marsh, where there was plenty of water, which frogs love: the other in a lane some distance away, where all the water to be had was that which lay in the ruts after rain. The Marsh Frog warned his friend and pressed him to come and live with him in the marsh, for he would find his quarters there far more comfortable and—what was still more important—more safe.

But the other refused, saying that he could not bring himself to move from a place to which he had become accustomed. A few days afterwards a heavy waggon came down the lane, and he was crushed to death under the wheels.

Do nothing without a regard to the consequences.

115. The Ass,the Cock, and the Lion

An Ass and a Cock were in a cattle-pen together. Presently a Lion, who had been starving for days, came along and was just about to fall upon the Ass and make a meal of him when the Cock, rising to his full height and flapping his wings vigorously, uttered a tremendous crow. Now, if there is one thing that frightens a Lion, it is the crowing of a Cock: and this one had no sooner heard the noise than he fled.

The Ass was mightily elated at this, and thought that, if the Lion couldn't face a Cock, he would be still less likely to stand up to an Ass: so he ran out and pursued him. But when the two had got well out of sight and hearing of the Cock, the Lion suddenly turned upon the Ass and ate him up.

False confidence often leads to disaster.

116. The Flea and the Ox

A Flea once said to an Ox, "How comes it that a big strong fellow like you is content to serve mankind, and do all their hard work for them, while I, who am no bigger than you see, live on their bodies and drink my fill of their blood, and never do a stroke for it all?"

To which the Ox replied, "Men are very kind to me, and so I am grateful to them: they feed and house me well, and every now and then they show their fondness for me by patting me on the head and neck." "They'd pat me, too," said the Flea, "if I let them: but I take good care they don't, or there would be nothing left of me."

A reward for one might be destruction for another.

117. The Stag in the Ox-Stall

A Stag, chased from his lair by the hounds, took refuge in a farmyard, and, entering a stable where a number of oxen were stalled, thrust himself under a pile of hay in a vacant stall, where he lay concealed, all but the tips of his horns. Presently one of the Oxen said to him, "What has induced you to come in here? Aren't you aware of the risk you are running of being captured by the herdsmen?"

To which he replied, "Pray let me stay for the present. When night comes I shall easily escape under cover of the dark." In the course of the afternoon more than one of the farm-hands came in, to attend to the wants of the cattle, but not one of them noticed the presence of the Stag, who accordingly began to congratulate himself on his escape and to express his gratitude to the Oxen. "We wish you well," said the one who had spoken before, "but you are not out of danger yet. If the master comes, you will certainly be found out, for nothing ever escapes his keen eyes."

Presently, sure enough, in he came, and made a great to-do about the way the Oxen were kept. "The beasts are starving," he cried; "here, give them more hay, and put plenty of litter under them." As he spoke, he seized an armful himself from the pile where the Stag lay concealed, and at once detected him. Calling his men, he had him seized at once and killed for the table.

What is safety to one is not always safety to another.

118. The Wolf, the Fox, and the Ape

A Wolf charged a Fox with theft, which he denied, and the case was brought before an Ape to be tried. When he had heard the evidence on both sides, the Ape gave judg-

ment as follows: "I do not think," he said, "that you, O Wolf, ever lost what you claim; but all the same I believe that you, Fox, are guilty of the theft, in spite of all your denials."

The dishonest get no credit, even if they act honestly.

119. The Wolf and the Sheep

A Wolf had been hurt in a fight with a Bear. He was unable to move and could not satisfy his hunger and thirst. A Sheep passed by near his hiding place, and the Wolf called to him.

"Please fetch me a drink of water," he begged, "that might give me strength enough so I can get me some solid food."

"Solid food!" said the Sheep. "That means me, I suppose. If I should bring you a drink, it would only serve to wash me down your throat. Don't talk to me about a drink!"

A knave's hypocrisy is easily seen through.

120. The Swan

The Swan is said to sing but once in its life—when it knows that it is about to die. A certain man, who had heard of the song of the Swan, one day saw one of these birds for sale in the market, and bought it and took it home with him. A few days later he had some friends to dinner, and produced the Swan, and bade it sing for their entertainment: but the Swan remained silent.

In course of time, when it was growing old, it became aware of its approaching end and broke into a sweet, sad song. When its owner heard it, he said angrily, "If the creature only sings when it is about to die, what a fool I was that day I wanted to hear its song! I ought to have wrung its neck instead of merely inviting it to sing."

A man cannot be too careful of what he does, where the life of any creature is in question.

121. The Cobbler Turned Doctor

A very unskilful Cobbler, finding himself unable to make a living at his trade, gave up mending boots and took to doctoring instead. He gave out that he had the secret of a universal antidote against all poisons, and acquired no small reputation, thanks to his talent for puffing himself. One day, however, he fell very ill; and the King of the country bethought him that he would test the value of his remedy.

Calling, therefore, for a cup, he poured out a dose of the antidote, and, under pretence of mixing poison with it, added a little water, and commanded him to drink it. Terrified by the fear of being poisoned, the Cobbler confessed that he knew nothing about medicine, and that his antidote was worthless. Then the King summoned his subjects and addressed them as follows: "What folly could be greater than yours? Here is this Cobbler to whom no one will send his boots to be mended, and yet you have not hesitated to entrust him with your lives!"

Beware of those not trained in their craft.

122. Mercury and the Sculptor

Mercury was very anxious to know in what estimation he was held by mankind; so he disguised himself as a man and walked into a Sculptor's studio, where there were a number of statues finished and ready for sale. Seeing a statue of Jupiter among the rest, he inquired the price of it.

"A crown," said the Sculptor. "Is that all?" said he, laughing; "and" (pointing to one of Juno) "how much is that one?" "That," was the reply, "is half a crown." "And how much might you be wanting for that one over there, now?" he continued, pointing to a statue of himself. "That one?" said the Sculptor; "Oh, I'll throw him in for nothing if you'll buy the other two."

Don't overvalue yourself.

123. The Runaway Slave

A Slave, being discontented with his lot, ran away from his master. He was soon missed by the latter, who lost no time in mounting his horse and setting out in pursuit of the fugitive. He presently came up with him, and the Slave, in the hope of avoiding capture, slipped into a treadmill and hid himself there.

"Aha," said his master, "that's the very place for you, my man!"

The result of our conduct is not predict.

124. The Trees and the Axe

A Woodman went into the forest and begged of the Trees the favour of a handle for his Axe. The principal Trees at once agreed to so modest a request, and unhesitatingly gave him a young ash sapling, out of which he fashioned the handle he desired.

No sooner had he done so than he set to work to fell the noblest Trees in the wood. When they saw the use to which he was putting their gift, they cried, "Alas! alas! We are undone, but we are ourselves to blame. The little we gave has cost us all: had we not sacrificed the rights of the ash, we might ourselves have stood for ages."

In yielding the rights of others, we may endanger our own.

125. The Dog and the Shadow

A Dog was crossing a plank bridge over a stream with a piece of meat in his mouth, when he happened to see his own reflection in the water. He thought it was another dog with a piece of meat twice as big; so he let

go his own, and flew at the other dog to get the larger piece.

But, of course, all that happened was that he got neither; for one was only a shadow, and the other was carried away by the current.

If you covet all, you may lose all.

126. The Lion and the Hare

A Lion found a Hare sleeping in her form, and was just going to devour her when he caught sight of a passing stag. Dropping the Hare, he at once made for the bigger game; but finding, after a long chase, that he could not overtake the stag, he abandoned the attempt and came back for the Hare. When he reached the spot, however, he found she was nowhere to be seen, and he had to go without his dinner.

"It serves me right," he said; "I should have been content with what I had got, instead of hankering after a better prize."

Take the opportunity at hand.

127. The Ass and the Dog

An Ass and a Dog were on their travels together, and, as they went along, they found a sealed packet lying on the ground. The Ass picked it up, broke the seal, and found it contained some writing, which he proceeded to read out aloud to the Dog.

As he read on it turned out to be all about grass and barley and hay—in short, all the kinds of fodder that Asses are fond of. The Dog was a good deal bored with listening to all this, till at last his impatience got the better of him, and he cried, "Just skip a few pages, friend, and see if there isn't something about meat and bones." The Ass glanced all through the packet, but found nothing of the sort, and said so.

Then the Dog said in disgust, "Oh, throw it away, do: what's the good of a thing like that?"

Have patience, and endure.

128. The Heifer and the Ox

A Heifer went up to an Ox, who was straining hard at the plough, and sympathised with him in a rather patronising sort of way on the necessity of his having to work so hard.

Not long afterwards there was a festival in the village and every one kept holiday: but, whereas the Ox was turned loose into the pasture, the Heifer was seized and led off to sacrifice.

"Ah," said the Ox, with a grim smile, "I see now why you were allowed to have such an idle time: it was because you were always intended for the altar."

The lives of the idle can best be sacrificed.

129. The Wasp and the Snake

A Wasp settled on the head of a Snake, and not only stung him several times, but clung obstinately to the head of his victim. Maddened with pain the Snake tried every means he could think of to get rid of the creature, but without success.

At last he became desperate, and crying, "Kill you I will, even at the cost of my own life," he laid his head with the Wasp on it under the wheel of a passing waggon, and they both perished together.

As a last resort take your enemy with you.

130. The Bear and the Fox

A Bear was once bragging about his generous feelings, and saying how refined he was compared with other animals. There is, in fact, a tradition that a Bear will never touch a dead body. A Fox, who heard him talking in this strain, smiled and said, "My friend, when you are hungry, I only wish you would confine your attention to the dead and leave the living alone."

A hypocrite deceives no one but himself.

131. The Lioness and the Vixen

A Lioness and a Vixen were talking together about their young, as mothers will, and saying how healthy and well-grown they were, and what beautiful coats they had, and how they were the image of their parents.

"My litter of cubs is a joy to see," said the Fox; and then she added, rather maliciously, "But I notice you never have more than one." "No," said the Lioness grimly, "but that one's a lion."

Quality, not quantity.

132. The Lion in Love

A Lion fell deeply in love with the daughter of a cottager and wanted to marry her; but her father was unwilling to give her to so fearsome a husband, and yet didn't want to offend the Lion; so he hit upon the following expedient.

He went to the Lion and said, "I think you will make a very good husband for my daughter: but I cannot consent to your union unless you let me draw your teeth and pare your nails, for my daughter is terribly afraid of them."

The Lion was so much in love that he readily agreed that this should be done. When once, however, he was thus disarmed, the Cottager was afraid of him no longer, but drove him away with his club.

Love can blind even the wildest.

133. The Owl and the Birds

The Owl is a very wise bird; and once, long ago, when the first oak sprouted in the forest, she called all the other Birds together and said to them, "You see this tiny tree? If you take my advice, you will destroy it now when it is small: for when it grows big, the mistletoe will appear upon it, from which birdlime will be prepared for your destruction."

Again, when the first flax was sown, she said to them, "Go and eat up that seed, for it is the seed of the flax, out of which men will one day make nets to catch you."

Once more, when she saw the first archer, she warned the Birds that he was their deadly enemy, who would wing his arrows

with their own feathers and shoot them. But they took no notice of what she said: in fact, they thought she was rather mad, and laughed at her.

When, however, everything turned out as she had foretold, they changed their minds and conceived a great respect for her wisdom. Hence, whenever she appears, the Birds attend upon her in the hope of hearing something that may be for their good.

She, however, gives them advice no longer, but sits moping and pondering on the folly of her kind.

Destroy the seed of evil, or it will grow up to your ruin.

134. The Walnut Tree

A Walnut tree, which grew by the roadside, bore every year a plentiful crop of nuts. Every one who passed by pelted its branches with sticks and stones, in order to bring down the fruit, and the tree suffered severely. "It is hard," it cried, "that the very persons who enjoy my fruit should thus reward me with insults and blows."

You always hurt the one you love.

135. The Olive Tree and the Fig Tree

An Olive Tree taunted a Fig Tree with the loss of her leaves at a certain season of the year. "You," she said, "lose your leaves every autumn, and are bare till the spring: whereas I, as you see, remain green and flourishing all the year round."

Soon afterwards there came a heavy fall of snow, which settled on the leaves of the Olive so that she bent and broke under the weight; but the flakes fell harmlessly through the bare branches of the Fig, which survived to bear many another crop.

Brag and nature may bring you down.

136. The Man and His Two Sweethearts

A Man of middle age, whose hair was turning grey, had two Sweethearts, an old woman and a young one. The elder of the two didn't like having a lover who looked so much younger than herself; so, whenever he came to see her, she used to pull the dark hairs out of his head to make him look old. The younger, on the other hand, didn't like him to look so much older than herself, and took every opportunity of pulling out the grey hairs, to make him look young.

Between them, they left not a hair in his head, and he became perfectly bald.

Those who seek to please everybody please nobody.

137. The Apes and the Two Travellers

Two men were travelling together, one of whom never spoke the truth, whereas the other never told a lie: and they came in the course of their travels to the land of Apes. The King of the Apes, hearing of their arrival, ordered them to be brought before him; and by way of impressing them with his magnificence, he received them sitting on a throne, while the Apes, his subjects, were ranged in long rows on either side of him.

When the Travellers came into his presence he asked them what they thought of him as a King. The lying Traveller said, "Sire, every one must see that you are a most noble and mighty monarch." "And what do you think of my subjects?" continued the King.

"They," said the Traveller, "are in every way worthy of their royal master." The Ape was so delighted with his answer that he gave him a very handsome present. The other Traveller thought that if his companion was rewarded so splendidly for telling a lie, he himself would certainly receive a still greater reward for telling the truth; so, when the Ape turned to him and said, "And what, sir, is your opinion?" he replied, "I think you are a very fine Ape, and all your subjects are fine Apes too."

The King of the Apes was so enraged at his reply that he ordered him to be taken away and clawed to death.

The truth often hurts.

138. The Rich Man and the Tanner

A Rich Man took up his residence next door to a Tanner, and found the smell of the tan-yard so extremely unpleasant that he told him he must go.

The Tanner delayed his departure, and the Rich Man had to speak to him several times about it; and every time the Tanner said he was making arrangements to move very shortly.

This went on for some time, till at last the Rich Man got so used to the smell that he ceased to mind it, and troubled the Tanner with his objections no more.

One can get used to most anything.

139. The Pomegranate, the Apple Tree, and the Bramble

A Pomegranate and an Apple tree were disputing about the quality of their fruits, and each claimed that its own was the better of the two. High words passed between them, and a violent quarrel was imminent, when a Bramble impudently poked its head out of a neighbouring hedge and said, “There, that’s enough, my friends; don’t let us quarrel.”

Everyone thinks themselves the best.

140. The Traveller and His Dog

A Traveller was about to start on a journey, and said to his Dog, who was stretching himself by the door, "Come, what are you yawning for? Hurry up and get ready: I mean you to go with me." But the Dog merely wagged his tail and said quietly, "I'm ready, master: it's you I'm waiting for."

The slacker often blames delay on the more active.

141. The Farmer and His Dogs

A Farmer was snowed up in his farmstead by a severe storm, and was unable to go out and procure provisions for himself and his family. So he first killed his sheep and used them for food; then, as the storm still continued, he killed his goats; and, last of all, as the weather showed no signs of improving, he was compelled to kill his oxen and eat them. When his Dogs saw the various animals being killed and eaten in turn, they said to one another, "We had better get out of this or we shall be the next to go!"

He is not to be trusted as a friend
who mistreats his own family.

142. The Eagle and His Captor

A Man once caught an Eagle, and after clipping his wings turned him loose among the fowls in his hen-house, where he moped in a corner, looking very dejected and forlorn.

After a while his Captor was glad enough to sell him to a neighbour, who took him home and let his wings grow again. As soon as he had recovered the use of them, the Eagle flew out and caught a hare, which he brought home and presented to his benefactor. A fox observed this, and said to the Eagle, "Don't waste your gifts on him! Go and give them to the man who first caught you; make him your friend, and then perhaps he won't catch you and clip your wings a second time."

Favor those who do you kindness.

143. The Snake and Jupiter

A Snake suffered a good deal from being constantly trodden upon by man and beast, owing partly to the length of his body and partly to his being unable to raise himself above the surface of the ground: so he went and complained to Jupiter about the risks to which he was exposed. But Jupiter had little sympathy for him.

"I dare say," said he, "that if you had bitten the first that trod on you, the others would have taken more trouble to look where they put their feet."

If you receive a gift you must befriend the giver.

144. The Bundle of Sticks

A certain Father had a family of Sons, who were forever quarreling among themselves. No words he could say did the least good, so he cast about in his mind for some very striking example that should make them see that discord would lead them to misfortune.

One day when the quarreling had been much more violent than usual and each of the Sons was moping in a surly manner, he asked one of them to bring him a bundle of sticks. Then handing the bundle to each of his Sons in turn he told them to try to break it. But although each one tried his best, none was able to do so.

The Father then untied the bundle and

gave the sticks to his Sons to break one by one. This they did very easily.

"My Sons," said the Father, "do you not see how certain it is that if you agree with each other and help each other, it will be impossible for your enemies to injure you? But if you are divided among yourselves, you will be no stronger than a single stick in that bundle."

In unity is strength.

145. The Cat and the Cock

A Cat pounced on a Cock, and cast about for some good excuse for making a meal off him, for Cats don't as a rule eat Cocks, and she knew she ought not to. At last she said, "You make a great nuisance of yourself at night by crowing and keeping people awake: so I am going to make an end of you."

But the Cock defended himself by say-

ing that he crowed in order that men might wake up and set about the day's work in good time, and that they really couldn't very well do without him. "That may be," said the Cat, "but whether they can or not, I'm not going without my dinner"; and she killed and ate him.

The want of a good excuse never kept
a villain from crime.

146. The Lamb Chased by a Wolf

A Wolf was chasing a Lamb, which took refuge in a temple. The Wolf urged it to come out of the precincts, and said, "If you don't, the priest is sure to catch you and offer you up in sacrifice on the altar."

To which the Lamb replied, "Thanks, I think I'll stay where I am: I'd rather be sacrificed any day than be eaten up by a Wolf."

It is safer to be among friends than enemies.

147. The Charcoal-Burner and the Fuller

There was once a Charcoal-burner who lived and worked by himself. A Fuller, however, happened to come and settle in the same neighbourhood; and the Charcoal-burner, having made his acquaintance and finding he was an agreeable sort of fellow, asked him if he would come and share his house: "We shall get to know one another better that way," he said, "and, beside, our household expenses will be diminished."

The Fuller thanked him, but replied, "I couldn't think of it, sir: why, everything I take such pains to whiten would be blackened in no time by your charcoal."

Like will draw like.

148. The Slave and the Lion

A Slave ran away from his master, by whom he had been most cruelly treated, and, in order to avoid capture, betook himself into the desert. As he wandered about in search of food and shelter, he came to a cave, which he entered and found to be unoccupied. Really, however, it was a Lion's den, and almost immediately, to the horror of the wretched fugitive, the Lion himself appeared.

The man gave himself up for lost: but, to his utter astonishment, the Lion, instead of springing upon him and devouring him, came and fawned upon him, at the same time whining and lifting up his paw. Observing it to be much swollen and inflamed, he examined it and found a large thorn embedded in the ball of the foot. He accordingly removed it and dressed the wound as well as he could: and in course of time it healed up completely. The Lion's gratitude was unbounded; he looked upon the man as his friend, and they shared the cave for some time together.

A day came, however, when the Slave began to long for the society of his fellow-men, and he bade farewell to the Lion and returned to the town. Here he was presently recognised and carried off in chains to his former master, who resolved to make an example of him, and ordered that he should be thrown to the beasts at the next public spectacle in the theatre.

On the fatal day the beasts were loosed into the arena, and among the rest a Lion of huge bulk and ferocious aspect; and then the wretched Slave was cast in among them. What was the amazement of the spectators, when the Lion after one glance bounded up to him and lay down at his feet with every expression of affection and delight! It was his old friend of the cave! The audience clamoured that the Slave's life should be spared: and the governor of the town, marvelling at such gratitude and fidelity in a beast, decreed that both should receive their liberty.

Kindness never goes unrewarded.

149. Mercury and the Man Bitten by an Ant

A Man once saw a ship go down with all its crew, and commented severely on the injustice of the gods. "They care nothing for a man's character," said he, "but let the good and the bad go to their deaths together."

There was an ant-heap close by where he was standing, and, just as he spoke, he was bitten in the foot by an Ant. Turning in a temper to the ant-heap he stamped upon it and crushed hundreds of unoffending ants.

Suddenly Mercury appeared, and belaboured him with his staff, saying as he did so, "You villain, where's your nice sense of justice now?"

Act as you profess to believe.

150. A Fisherman's Good Luck

A Fisherman had been a long while at work without catching any thing, and so in great trouble and despair, he resolv'd to take up his tackle, and be gone: but in that very instant a great fish leapt into the boat, and by this providence he made a tolerable day on't.

Patience has its own reward.

memo

memo

memo

memo

THE CLASSIC
An Imprint of MIRBOOK COMPANY Publishing Co,.
2F, 12 Seongmisan-ro 32-gil, Mapo-gu, Seoul, South Korea
T; +82 2 3141 4421 | F; +82 2 3141 4428
E-mail; sanhonjinju@naver.com

Aesop's Fables 2
By Aesop | Arthur Rackham

Published by MIRBOOK COMPANY Co,.